MIA HAMM
GOOD AS GOLD

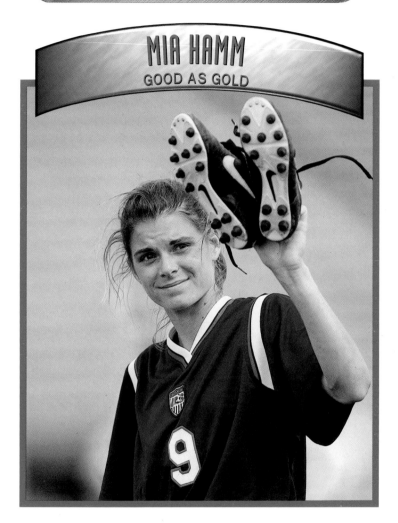

BY MARK STEWART

℘ Children's Press®
A Division of Grolier Publishing
New York London Hong Kong Sydney
Danbury, Connecticut

Photo Credits

Photographs ©: Allsport USA: 9, 13, 30, 33, 45 left (David Cannon),32(StephenDunn) 15, 44 right (Andy Lyons), 27, 28 (Rick Stewart); Andrew Cline Photography: 24; AP/Wide World Photos: 38 (Adam Nadel); Archive Photos: 35 (Reuters/Pierre Ducharme); Hugh Morton: 18; Simon Bruty: 10; 25; SportsChrome East/West: 21, 41, right, 47 (John Todd), 39 (Bob Tringali), cover, 3, 6, 36, 43, 46 (Rob Tringali Jr.); UNC/Sports Info: 17,44 left; University of North Carolina: 22.

Visit Children's Press on the Internet at:
http://publishing.grolier.com

Library of Congress Cataloging-in-Publication Data

Stewart, Mark.
 Mia Hamm : good as gold / by Mark Stewart.
  p. cm. — (Sports stars)
  Includes index.
  Summary: A biography of one of the top female soccer players in the world, Mia Hamm, who helped the United States win a gold medal in soccer in the 1996 Olympics.
  ISBN 0-516-21221-4 (lib.bdg)   0-516-26487-7 (pbk.)
  1. Hamm, Mia, 1972– —Juvenile literature. 2. Soccer players— United States—Biography—Juvenile literature. [1. Hamm, Mia, 1972– . 2. Soccer players. 3. Women—Biography.] I. Title. II. Series.
GV942.7.H27S74 1999
796.334'092—dc21
[B]   98–45308
               CIP
               AC

CONTENTS

★ 1 ★

NEAT FEET

Stephanie Hamm always believed that her daughter, Mia, would achieve fame with her feet. A ballerina in her youth, she encouraged Mia to dance. Finally, when she thought Mia was ready, she took her to her first ballet class. "I hated it," laughs Mia. "I lasted one class!" Some, however, would say that Mia's mom got the last laugh. After all, Mia now has the most famous feet in women's sports. The big breakthrough came not in the dance studio, but on the soccer field. The daughter of Bill Hamm, an Air Force pilot, Mia lived on a base in Florence, Italy, when she was little, and as early as age one she was toddling into soccer games.

★ ★ ★

In 1977, after the family moved to Texas, Bill and Stephanie adopted Garrett, an 8-year-old Thai-American orphan. Mia and Garrett became inseparable. Whatever her new brother did, five-year-old Mia wanted to do. Garrett's favorite sport was soccer; soon it was Mia's, too. Bill Hamm was also a big fan of the game. In fact, soccer soon became the most popular game in the Hamm house. When Mia was not playing or watching her siblings play, she would sit in the living room, transfixed by soccer games broadcast on the local Spanish-language television stations.

Mia had learned a lot about soccer by the time she began playing seriously, and it showed in her ability to score. She could change speed and direction quickly when the other kids were still getting tangled up in their own feet. Mia could kick the ball hard with either foot, and she could make it do things in the air, like curve and dip around the goaltender. And she always seemed to be where the ball was, both on offense and defense. She truly had a special gift for the game.

Mia's ball-controls skills have been superb since she was a little girl.

Mia also enjoyed the freedom soccer offered. From the time she could walk, she was always running around the house or climbing things she was not supposed to—often to shouts of "No!" from her parents. "Soccer was different," she says. "On the field, I could run fast and jump high and kick the ball as hard as I could and all these great things. And it was actually encouraged!"

Mia is used to being double-teamed. She has been the best player on the field in almost every game she has ever played.

Throughout her childhood, Mia played against older kids, and she gained confidence and experience by trying new ideas and seeing how they worked. Win or lose, she rarely left the field without having taken something positive from the game. Soon soccer was everything to Mia. She was a highly emotional girl, but also very shy. Soccer let her express herself. "It made me who I am," Mia insists. "I was given a tremendous gift in terms of athleticism, and I believe I was given it for a reason. Maybe it was because I wasn't so confident in other areas."

By the time she enrolled in Notre Dame High School, in Wichita Falls, Texas, 14-year-old Mia was not only the star of the girl's team, she was better than anyone on the boys' varsity team. In fact, she was the top female player in the entire state. Mia first came to the attention of the U.S. Soccer Federation when John Cossaboon, coach of a special development team, saw her play in Texas. He then invited Anson Dorrance to come see Mia for himself.

$$\star\ \star\ \star$$

Dorrance, the coach of the powerhouse University of North Carolina Tar Heels, was the most influential figure in women's soccer. His team had already captured three NCAA championships, and there would be many more to come. Cossaboon had been so enthusiastic in his description of Mia that Dorrance suspected he was exaggerating. He asked that his friend not point out the young star—if she was as good as he claimed, it would be obvious.

The first time Mia touched the ball, Dorrance knew who she was. He watched as she dominated the game from her position at midfield. She was a fast and intelligent player, but what impressed him most was her natural feel for the game. When Mia was on the attack, she shed defenders without missing a beat. When a team hemmed her in with two or three players, she could pass the ball right onto the foot of a teammate. To Dorrance, this was the most exciting thing about Mia's ability. He knew she would run into better

**Mia's knack for weaving through opposing defenses was one
of the first things to catch Anson Dorrance's eye.**

defenders as she progressed in soccer, yet she already had the skills to handle these challenges.

Dorrance asked Mia to play in the 1987 U.S. Soccer Federation tournament in New Orleans, Louisiana. It would be her first time competing with and against better players—including members of the women's national team, which he had helped to form two years earlier. After some nervous moments, Mia performed brilliantly and distinguished herself as one of the top midfielders in the country. Also, she learned an important lesson about the kind of conditioning it would take to reach the next level. "It was a nightmare," Mia remembers. "When I first did fitness with the national team, I thought I'd die. I would cry half the time."

Mia also made a new friend in New Orleans, named Kris Lilly. She was busy rewriting the high-school record books across the country in Wilton, Connecticut. They decided it would be fun to play together for Coach Dorrance after they graduated. Mia returned from the tournament more passionate than ever about soccer. She told her parents that she wanted to earn a scholarship to the University of North Carolina, and someday win a world championship. At the time, there was no Women's World Cup, and the sport was not part of the Olympics, so there really was no

such thing as a championship. Still, a goal was a goal. And where goals were involved, Mia's impossible to stop.

No one in soccer is more focused on her goals than Mia.

★ 2 ★

TEAM PLAYER

Before Mia's junior year in high school, Bill Hamm was transferred again. This time the family moved to Burke, Virginia. Mia enrolled at Lake Braddock Secondary School and began what would be her first of two All-American seasons there. At the same time, she established herself as one of the key players on the national squad, teaming with Michelle Akers, Carin Gabarra, Joy Fawcett, Carla Overbeck, and her friend, Kris Lilly, to form the core of a terrific young team. She played in a total of 15 games for Team USA in 1987 and 1988, which resulted in 7 wins, 5 losses and 3 ties. In other words, there was plenty of room for improvement. After graduating from South Lakes in 1989, Mia took

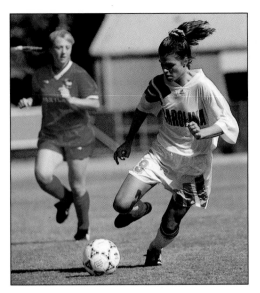

The addition of Mia to the Tar Heels in 1989 made a great team even better.

time off from the national team to concentrate on college. She was off to Chapel Hill to play for Anson Dorrance, just as she had planned.

Mia joined a team already considered the country's best. Since the NCAA began holding its women's championship tournament in the fall of 1982, the University of North Carolina had won 6 times in 7 seasons. The team already had a strong midfield and back line, so Dorrance moved Mia up to forward, where the Tar Heels could get the full benefits of her goal-scoring skills. She was UNC's "finisher" in 1989, scoring 21 goals in 23 games. In the season-ending Atlantic Coast Conference Tournament, she was named Most

Valuable Player. Then UNC went on to win the NCAA championship.

Mia's sophomore year was even better. She scored 24 goals and was credited with 19 assists, for a total of 67 points. This figure led all college players. Mia finished 1990 as the ACC Player of the Year and a first-team All-American, and the Tar Heels won another NCAA championship.

Then Mia had to make a big decision.

FIFA, soccer's international governing body, was holding the first women's world championship that fall, in China. The number of women playing the game worldwide was exploding, and FIFA saw an opportunity to expand its influence in three important ways. First, by sanctioning women's soccer, it could greatly

Mia says the decision to leave UNC for Team USA was a difficult one.

increase its membership. Second, by holding the tournament in China, it could expose the game to a billion new fans. Third, if the United States did well it might generate enthusiasm for soccer in America, where it had always lagged behind the other sports.

Mia did not care about the politics; she just wanted to be a part of the big event. After all, this was her greatest dream. But rejoining the national team and training for the tournament would mean leaving school for a year. Mia did not want to let down her teammates. Dorrance—who was asked to coach Team USA in the tournament—made the decision easy for his star player. He told her to skip a year and then come back as a junior for her final two college seasons. Football players, he pointed out, do this all the time; it is called "red-shirting."

As a member of Team USA, Mia found herself part of a serious, committed group of veteran players ready to make a run at the world title. The squad with which she had played a few years earlier had really grown up, and was now an international power. Mia had grown up since

then, too—even though she was still the youngest
player in camp. The national team began its season
in April 1991, and played all summer and fall in
preparation for the November tournament in China.
When it began, the big favorite was Norway.

In the opener, against Sweden, Mia had to play
out of position, as an outside midfielder. She made
several mistakes, but redeemed herself by scoring
the game-winning goal. She scored again in the
next match—a 5–0 win against Brazil—and played
wonderfully as the team made it all the way to the
finals, where they faced the tough Norwegians.
In that match, Michelle Akers gave Team USA a
surprising 1–0 lead with a brilliant header that
brought the 65,000 fans in Guangzhou's Tianhe
Stadium to their feet. Norway knotted the contest
with a goal, and the two teams went toe-to-toe into
the game's closing minutes. Just when everyone
was getting ready for overtime, Akers spotted an
enemy defender getting ready to kick the ball back
to goalkeeper Reidun Seth. Akers darted between
the two, intercepted the weak pass, and blasted the

As the youngest member of Team USA in 1991, she helped win the world championship.

ball into an empty net. The team held on for dear life over the final three minutes, and ran off the field world champions.

Mia looks for an opening during a 1992 game. She returned to UNC for her junior season and scored a record 33 goals.

★ 3 ★

BACK TO SCHOOL

Mia returned to North Carolina a year older and a lot wiser. Her body was stronger and faster, and she was a much smarter player. When she was unleashed on college soccer, it was like watching a pro play with children. Mia led the Tar Heels to an undefeated season, scoring 32 goals in 25 games. Her 33 assists that year shattered the all-time collegiate record, and her 97 total points also eclipsed the old mark. In the NCAA Tournament, she set another record with 6 goals. Mia was named Player of the Year and was a unanimous choice as an All-American. She also won the Hermann Award as the nation's top female athlete.

Mia's balance and timing make her even more dangerous on a slippery field. In her final college season, she led UNC to a fourth national title.

In Mia's senior year, she led UNC to another NCAA championship. Though routinely shadowed—and often roughed-up—by opposing players, she still managed to score 26 times in 22 games. Once again, Mia was an All-American, NCAA Player of the Year, and winner of the Hermann Award. She walked away from Chapel Hill with a 92–1–2 record as a Tar Heel, and she owned just about every offensive mark in the books. Mia produced more goals (103), assists (72), and points (278) than anyone in the history of women's college soccer, and also established new career marks in these categories for the NCAA Tournament. What she remembers most about her Tar Heel days, though, is not all the awards, but the spirit on the team. "Each person's character and personality got to come out," Mia says. "It was an exciting and special group, and I'm glad I was a part of it."

Mia leaves opponents grasping at air. Her return to Team USA in 1994 resulted in her first U.S. Soccer Female Athlete of the Year award.

Mia returned to the national team in the spring of 1994 and netted 10 goals in 9 games. Six of those goals came during the qualifying tournament for the Women's World Cup, which FIFA had scheduled for 1995 in Sweden. Team USA finished the 1994 season with a smashing 12–1 record, and Mia was named Female Athlete of the Year by the U.S. Soccer Federation.

The following season began with great hope, but ended in disappointment. Mia continued to play well, with 19 goals and 18 assists in 21 games, but coach Tony DiCicco (who had taken over for Coach Dorrance in 1994) had a difficult time fielding a healthy team, as several Team USA players suffered injuries. At the World Cup, Mia actually had to play goalie during a game against Denmark when DiCicco ran out of substitutes! The team managed to make it to the semifinals, but then lost to Norway, 1–0. Team USA had to settle for third.

Mia has been Team USA's top player since 1994.

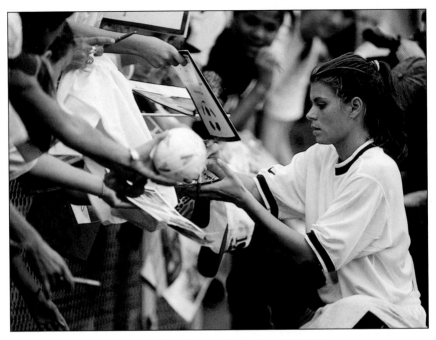

Mia signs autographs for fans after the 1995 Women's World Cup.

For four years Mia and her teammates had looked forward to the first official Women's World Cup, and it was a big disappointment to lose. The leading players and the coaching staff got together and decided from that day on, they would try to improve every game. "We renewed our intensity," Mia recalls, "and geared it towards Atlanta in 1996."

★ 4 ★

GOOD AS GOLD

The 1996 season promised to be the greatest ever for women's soccer. For the first time, the sport would be an official event in the Olympics, and every country in the world was gearing up to go for the gold medal. With the summer games to be held in and around Atlanta, Georgia, Team USA had home-field advantage. To maintain that edge, Team USA scheduled 19 games with top international competition, beginning in January. The team won 18 of those matches. Heading into the Olympics, the players were at the top of their games. And everyone was talking about Mia Hamm.

Mia bursts past a defender during the 1996 Olympics.

★ ★ ★

After two phenomenal seasons, Mia was
now considered the best player in the world. She
combined balance, speed, quickness, and power
in a way no other woman ever had. Mia had all
of the individual skills, but played within the
team concept. If she believed a 30-yard sprint
to the goal was the best play, she would weave
her way through the defense. But if Mia saw
Michelle Akers or Tiffeny Milbrett slicing toward
the net, she would hit them with perfect passes.
Opponents often changed their defensive
schemes hoping to shut Mia down, and it was
not unusual for her to be fouled five or more
times a game. Indeed, she was a marked woman.

This was especially true in Team USA's first-
round victories over Denmark and Sweden. Mia
was tripped, held, and shoved repeatedly during
these games. With seven minutes to go against
Sweden, she slammed into goalie Annelie Nilsson
and sprained her ankle. This was a serious injury
for Mia, who relies on bursts of speed to set
up her attack. With Norway coming up in the

semifinals, the Americans suddenly were considered underdogs. Though Mia could play, she would not be a major factor.

Every one of the 64,000-plus fans filing into Sanford Stadium for the Norway match was thinking the same thing: it was time to see just

Mia strains to stay on her feet after being fouled.

Mia leads Team USA in its Olympic game against Norway.

how good a *team* Team USA had become. After
90 minutes, the fans had their answer. The game
was knotted 1–1, with Akers scoring the team's
lone goal and Joy Fawcett and Carla Overbeck
playing brilliant defense in front of the acrobatic
goalkeeper, Briana Scurry. Coach DiCicco,
sensing the game might be won with fresh legs,
sent Shannon MacMillan on to the field to start
the overtime period. Four minutes later, she
scored the game-winner to put the United States
into the final.

With more than 76,000 fans cheering them on, Mia and her teammates took the field against China four days later for the final step of their long journey to the top. Team USA scored a pair of early goals and then held on for a 2–1 victory. Mia, who had to come out of the game, was overjoyed when the final gun sounded. Many times over the years, her teammates had looked to her to come through when it was time to pull out a tough win. After her injury, Mia felt as if she had let the team down. Now the whole world knew what she knew: every player on the squad could play big when they had to, especially in the biggest game of their lives.

In the locker room, the players giggled and screamed like little kids. They had not only won the gold medal in front of their friends and families, they had a great time doing it. Mia thought about the day, nine years earlier, when she first walked on to the field with the national team, and how much growing up they had done together. She thought about all of the places she had played, all of the friends she had made, and all of the people who had helped her along the way. She thought about Garrett, who was fighting a life-threatening illness, and how he had always picked her for his team in touch football when everyone else thought she was too small.

Mia celebrates an Olympic victory.

★ 5 ★

GROWING THE GAME

After the 1996 Olympics, Mia was the toast of soccer. She could be seen in television commercials and on magazine covers, and her name was fast becoming a household word. Women's soccer was also gaining ground. Team USA played in Australia, Germany, and Brazil during 1997, and in May two of its games were televised nationally. Rising to the occasion, Mia scored three goals in each contest. She scored on 12 other occasions during 1997, giving her a total of 18 goals in 16 games. For her efforts, Mia was named U.S. Soccer Federation Female Athlete of the Year for an unprecedented fourth consecutive season.

Mia shows off her 1998 ESPY award for Female Athlete of the Year.

What should have been a wonderful year, though, was filled with sadness. Garrett, who suffered from a rare blood disorder called aplastic anemia, received a life-saving bone marrow transplant in February. But complications set in, and he died in April. "I'd give up all of this in a heartbeat to have him back," says Mia of her fame and fortune. "Just to give him one more day or one more week. But I know Garrett wouldn't want that. . . . Now, no matter where I play, I feel Garrett is there."

Mia hit the field running in 1998. It was a season of new challenges and important goals. The year began on a high note as Team USA scored a 3–0 victory over Norway in the final of the International Women's Tournament. On March 17, Mia celebrated her 26th birthday with three goals against China in the prestigious Algarve Cup. A 4–1 loss to Norway two days later served as a wake-up call for Team USA, which rolled over the rest of its opponents all year long.

Mia dominates play during the 1998 Goodwill Games. Her five goals in the final two games brought a gold medal to Team USA.

In April, Mia registered a pair of goals and seven assists in two games against Argentina. In May, Mia's longtime teammate, Kris Lilly, played in her 125th international game, which gave her the all-time record for women's soccer. In June, Mia blasted three goals in a 20-minute span to beat Germany, the most-improved team in the world.

In July, Mia was dominant as Team USA won the gold medal at the Goodwill Games. Her three goals against Denmark in the semifinals boosted the national team into the final with China. Against the Chinese, Mia scored both goals in a 2–0 shutout. She finished the 1998 season with 20 goals and 20 assists in 20 games, and became the all-time leading goal-scorer in the history of U.S. soccer, breaking the record set by Michelle Akers. "She's the ultimate professional," says Mia of Michelle. "She does so much for the sport and I'm so proud to be her teammate. I hope that some of that rubs off on me."

Mia is surrounded by adoring fans.

Akers, an original member of the national team, which was formed in 1985, is now passing the torch of leadership to Mia. The game is more established now, but there is much more work to be done in order for women's soccer to grow. Mia and her teammates must be role models and ambassadors and teachers, yet they also have to keep winning. It makes for a very full schedule!

★ ★ ★

"It is something we take very seriously," says Mia, who believes the future of the women's game is bright. "I think we have a tremendous product on the field and individuals who can really sell the game."

As for her own special place in the sport, Mia downplays its importance. "We want to get girls out to the games," she says. "We want them to see the chemistry and the intensity. Our success is as a team, not me as an individual."

Mia might get an argument there. Anyone who has seen her play knows that much of her team's success is due to her outrageous ability and never-say-die attitude. Mia Hamm may be the ultimate team player, but she is also soccer's most amazing individual talent.

As a role model, Mia hopes to encourage girls to become more involved in sports.

C ☆ H ☆ R ☆ O ☆ N

1972   • March 17: Mia is born.

1987   • Mia is asked by Coach Anson Dorrance to play in the U.S. Soccer Federation Tournament in New Orleans, Louisiana. At age 15, she becomes the youngest member of Team USA.

1989   • Mia goes to the University of North Carolina to play soccer for Coach Dorrance. She is named Most Valuable Player in the Atlantic Coast Conference Tournament.

       • UNC wins the NCAA Championship.

1990   • Mia leads all college players with 67 points. She finishes the season as the ACC's Player of the Year and a First-Team All-American.

1991   • Mia leaves college for one year to join Team USA .

O ⋆ L ⋆ O ⋆ G ⋆ Y

1992
- Mia returns to college and propels North Carolina to an undefeated season, leading the nation with 32 goals in 25 games. She wins the Hermann Award as the nation's top female athlete.

1993
- Mia ends her Tar Heels days with more goals (103), assists (72), and points (278) than anyone in the history of college soccer.

1994
- Mia wins the Broderick Award as the NCAA's top female athlete.

1996
- Mia leads Team USA to the Olympic gold medal in Atlanta, Georgia.

1998
- Mia leads Team USA to the gold medal at the Goodwill Games. She scores her 100th career goal vs. Russia on September 18th, and finishes the season as the all-time leading goal-scorer in the history of U.S. soccer.

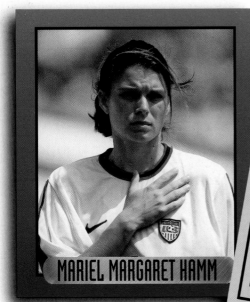

MARIEL MARGARET HAMM

MARIEL MARGARET HAMM

Date of Birth **March 17, 1972**

Place of Birth **Selma, Alabama**

Height **5′ 5″**

Weight **125 pounds**

Uniform Number **9**

College **University of North Carolina**

Championships
Four-Time NCAA Champion
1991 World Champion

Honors
Olympic Gold Medalist
Team USA All-Time Scoring Leader
1994-98 US Soccer Female Athlete of the Year
1997 ESPN Female Athlete of the Year
1994 Broderick Award Winner
1992 & 93 Hermann Award Winner
1992 & 93 NCAA Player of the Year
Three-Time College All-American
Two-Time High School All-American
Youngest Ever Team USA Member

★ ★ ★

ABOUT THE AUTHOR

Mark Stewart grew up in New York City in the 1960s and 1970s—when the Mets, Jets, and Knicks all had championship teams. As a child, Mark read everything about sports he could lay his hands on. Today, he is one of the busiest sportswriters around. Since 1990, he has written close to 500 sports stories for kids, including profiles on more than 200 athletes, past and present. A graduate of Duke University, Mark served as senior editor of *Racquet,* a national tennis magazine, and was managing editor of *Super News*, a sporting-goods industry newspaper. His syndicated newspaper column, *Mark My Words*, is read by sports fans nationwide. He is the author of every Grolier All-Pro Biography and 17 titles in the Children's Press Sports Stars series.